Ohio

BY ANN HEINRICHS

Content Adviser: Sharon Antle, Chief of Education Programs, Ohio Historical Society, Columbus, Ohio

Reading Adviser: Dr. Linda D. Labbo, Department of Reading Education, College of Education, The University of Georgia

COMPASS POINT BOOKS ✦ MINNEAPOLIS, MINNESOTA

Compass Point Books
3722 West 50th Street, #115
Minneapolis, MN 55410

Visit Compass Point Books on the Internet at *www.compasspointbooks.com*
or e-mail your request to *custserv@compasspointbooks.com*

On the cover: Olins covered bridge, Ashtabula County

Photographs ©: Carl A. Stimac/The Image Finders, cover, 1; William A. Holmes/The Image Finders, 3, 36; Unicorn Stock Photos/Andre Jenny, 5, 30, 45; PhotoDisc, 6, 41; Jim Baron/The Image Finders, 7, 13, 40, 44 (bottom left), 48; Unicorn Stock Photos/Jeff Greenberg, 8, 47; Photo Network/David Davis, 9; Tom Till, 10, 42; Robert McCaw, 12, 43; Unicorn Stock Photos/Gary Randall, 14; Stock Montage, 15, 16, 25; Bettmann/Corbis, 17, 29; Hulton/Archive by Getty Images, 18, 24; North Wind Picture Archives, 19; NASA/Visuals Unlimited, 20, 46; Unicorn Stock Photos/Patti McConville, 21; Jeff Greenberg/The Image Finders, 23; Kevin Fleming/Corbis, 26; Susan Spetz/The Image Finders, 27; Chick Piper/Visuals Unlimited, 31; Sean Gallup/Getty Images, 32; William Holmes/The Image Finders, 33; Michael Evans/The Image Finders, 34, 38; Mark E. Gibson/The Image Finders, 37; Robesus, Inc, 43 (state flag); One Mile Up, Inc., 43 (state seal); Bill Leaman/The Image Finders, 44 (top left); Becky Luigart-Stayner/Corbis, 44 (bottom right).

Editors: E. Russell Primm, Emily J. Dolbear, and Catherine Neitge
Photo Researcher: Svetlana Zhurkina
Photo Selector: Linda S. Koutris
Designer: The Design Lab
Cartographer: XNR Productions, Inc.

Library of Congress Cataloging-in-Publication Data
Heinrichs, Ann.
    Ohio / by Ann Heinrichs.
        p. cm.— (This land is your land)
    Summary: Introduces the geography, history, government, people, culture, and attractions of Ohio.
    Includes bibliographical references (p.) and index.
    ISBN 0-7565-0316-7
    1. Ohio—Juvenile literature. [1. Ohio.] I. Title. II. Series: Heinrichs, Ann. This land is your land.
    F491.3.H45 2003
    977.1—dc21   2002010100

Table of Contents

The famous writer Charles Dickens visited Ohio in 1842. He called it "a beautiful country" with "promise of an abundant harvest." Dickens was right. Early settlers raised plentiful crops in Ohio's rich soil. Today, Ohio is still a top farming state. It's a leader in manufacturing, too.

Ohio's state **slogan** is "Ohio—So Much to Discover!" Soon you'll discover Ohio for yourself. Ohio's forests and rivers are great places to explore. So are its underground caves and its ancient **mounds.** Ohio is also the perfect place to learn about our history. Eight U.S. presidents came from Ohio. Visitors can see where they lived and worked. Rock and roll history comes to life in Ohio, too. It's the home of the Rock and Roll Hall of Fame.

Whatever your interests are, you'll agree: Ohio has so much to discover!

▲ A view of the Cleveland skyline, home to the Rock and Roll Hall of Fame (right)

Rivers, Forests, and Plains

Ohio is one of the nation's Midwestern states. It lies between Indiana on the west and Pennsylvania on the east. To the south is Kentucky. West Virginia curls around Ohio's southeastern corner. Michigan borders the northwest. Lake Erie, one of North America's five Great Lakes, lies north of Ohio.

Eastern Ohio is a beautiful, rugged region. Winding rivers cut through its steep hills. Dense forests and sparkling waterfalls add to its natural beauty. Many valuable minerals lie underground.

▲ **Ohio is a Midwestern state that is filled with places to explore and new things to discover.**

The rolling plains of western Ohio are known for their rich, dark soil. Farmers in the plains grow tons of corn, soybeans, and wheat. The major city on the eastern edge of this region is Columbus, the state capital.

Northern Ohio was once covered by Lake Erie. The lake left behind rich soil for farming. Cities along Lake Erie became industrial and shipping centers. They include Cleveland, Toledo, Akron, and Sandusky. Several small islands cluster in the lake near Sandusky. They provide ideal recreation and vacation spots.

▲ Lake Erie is one of the five Great Lakes and makes up Ohio's northern border.

Over the years, Lake Erie became badly polluted. Factory wastes drifted into the waters. Storms washed away the shoreline, too. The state has worked hard to clean up the lake and has brought it back to life.

▲ The Ohio River is a branch of the Mississippi and forms Ohio's southern border.

Ohio's southern border follows the Ohio River. Native Americans called the river *Ohio,* meaning "Great Water" or "Something Great." The word *Ohio* later became the whole state's name.

The Ohio River is a branch of the mighty Mississippi. That river was an important "highway" for explorers and

▲ Ohio forests are filled with colorful leaves in autumn.

settlers. Farmers shipped their goods on this waterway, too. The Scioto River is the Ohio's longest branch. Some of the Ohio's streams run underground. They have hollowed out huge underground caves.

Most of Ohio's forest trees are deciduous. This means they shed their leaves in the fall. Maples, beeches, hickories,

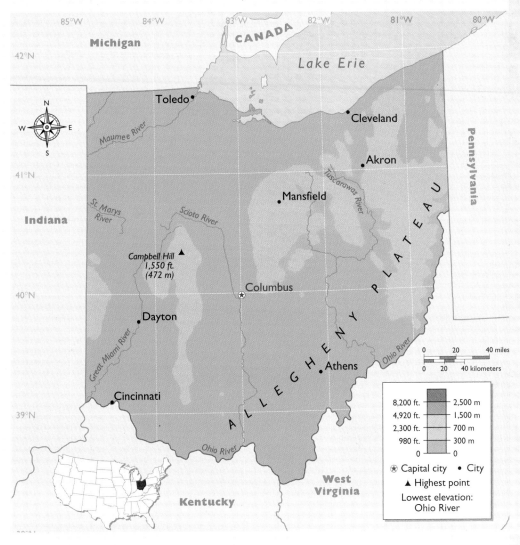

▲ A topographic map of Ohio

and oaks grow in these forests. The buckeye is the state tree. It is named for its nut, which looks like the eye of a buck, or male deer.

White-tailed deer roam through Ohio's woodlands.

Opossums, foxes, skunks, and rabbits scurry about on the forest floor. Squirrels share the treetops with chickadees, cardinals, and wrens.

▲ **This black-capped chickadee is one of many animals that live in Ohio's woodlands.**

▲ **Winters can be quite snowy in Ohio.**

Ohioans sometimes joke about the weather. "If you don't like the weather, wait five minutes. It will change." Ohio's winters can be quite cold and snowy. That's good news for skiers. They love northeastern Ohio for its heavy snowfalls. Summers, however, are warm and sunny. People drive for miles to see Ohio's colorful leaves in the fall.

Ancient peoples lived in Ohio around two thousand years ago. They were the Adena and the Hopewell peoples. They hunted, fished, and gathered wild berries. They traded their pottery and tools with people as far away as Mexico. Both groups built huge burial mounds and other **earthworks.** That's why they are sometimes called the Mound Builders.

▲ These burial mounds were built by the Hopewell Indians. Often, gifts of beads, bracelets, pots, and tools were buried with the dead.

René-Robert Cavelier, Sieur de La Salle, was probably the first European to set foot in Ohio. La Salle, a French explorer from Canada, arrived around 1670. First, France claimed the region. Then it passed to Great Britain in 1763 after the French and Indian Wars (1689–1763). The new United States took over Ohio after the Revolutionary War (1775–1783). Then, in 1787, Ohio became part of the vast Northwest Territory.

▲ René-Robert Cavelier, Sieur de La Salle

Pioneers from the eastern states founded Marietta in 1788. It became Ohio's first

▲ U.S. soldiers defeated nearly two thousand Indian warriors in the Battle of Fallen Timbers.

European settlement. Early settlers found many Native American villages. The villages belonged to the Miami, the Wyandot, the Shawnee, and the Delaware peoples. The Indians fought many battles to keep their land. After the Battle of Fallen Timbers in 1794, they lost most of Ohio.

▲ Pioneers traveling along the Ohio River

In 1803, Ohio became the seventeenth U.S. state. Its farmers raised wheat, corn, hogs, and cattle. They shipped their products on the Ohio River and Lake Erie. Ohioans dug canals to transport their goods, too.

Pioneer families stored grain in hollowed-out logs. They gathered wild herbs to make medicines. Soap was made from animal fat. Goose feathers made plump pillows and cozy **feather beds.** Neighbors got together to cook maple syrup and apple butter.

▲ These Ohio abolitionists were known as the Oberlin Rescuers.

Many Ohioans were **abolitionists.** They were against slavery. Some took part in the Underground Railroad, a secret system that helped runaway slaves escape to freedom. The Civil War (1861–1865) put an end to slavery at last.

Ohio cities were growing fast. Lake Erie ports shipped out coal, iron, and farm products. Many cities had busy factories, too. Some packed meat, ground flour, or refined oil. Others made rubber or steel. By 1900, Ohio was a leading industrial state.

The Great Depression of the 1930s was tough on Ohioans. Thousands of people were out of work. World War II (1939–1945) helped get them back on their feet. Ohio's farms and factories produced tons of war supplies.

▲ An ad for a rubber and tire company operating out of Ohio

Americans were glued to their television sets in June 1969. They watched Ohioan Neil Armstrong become the first human to walk on the moon. Earlier in 1962, Ohio **astronaut** John Glenn became the first American to **orbit** Earth.

Ohio saw many changes in the years to come. New industries came into the state. Many cities built new downtown areas. Others cleaned up their rivers and lakes. Ohioans are proud of their state today!

▲ **The first man to walk on the moon was Ohioan Neil Armstrong.**

Like most states, Ohio follows the example of the U.S. government. It has three branches of government—legislative, executive, and judicial. This is a good way to divide power. Each branch keeps an eye on the other two.

The legislative branch makes the state laws. Ohio's lawmakers serve in the general assembly. It has two sections—a thirty-three-member senate and a ninety-nine-member house of representatives.

The executive branch

▲ **Ohio state courthouse**

▲ **A geopolitical map of Ohio**

makes sure the laws are carried out. Ohio's governor is the

head of the executive branch. Ohioans vote to choose a

governor every four years. Other executive officers help the

governor. They include the lieutenant governor, secretary

of state, treasurer, auditor, and attorney general.

▲ This courthouse in Chester is the oldest one in Ohio.

Ohio's judges and courts make up the judicial branch. They decide whether someone has broken a law. Ohio's highest court is the state supreme court. Voters choose its seven judges.

The state is divided into eighty-eight counties. Counties may choose home rule. That means they can make their own charter, or statement, of freedoms and powers. Only Summit County has done this, however. County governments provide services and courts for citizens of the county.

Ohio has no towns! If a community has fewer than 5,000 people, it's a village. With 5,000 or more people, it's a city.

Ohioans are proud of their home-grown leaders. Seven U.S. presidents were born in Ohio, and an eighth president lived there. Also, Ohio astronaut John Glenn served in the U.S. Senate.

▲ Ohioan Ulysses S. Grant, Civil War hero and eighteenth U.S. president

What was life like before Thomas Edison? It was definitely darker and probably quieter! Edison invented electric light bulbs and record players. How about life before Orville and Wilbur Wright? It was slower! The Wright brothers flew the first airplane in 1903. Before Garrett Morgan, life was dangerous! He invented the traffic light in 1923.

These people were just a few of Ohio's inventors. They made our everyday life easier and more

▲ **Famous inventor Thomas Edison**

▲ Steel mills are a common sight in Ohio. The state is second only to Indiana in steel production.

interesting. Now factories keep busy making the great things they invented.

Ohio is a top manufacturing state. Its factories make cars and trucks, airplane parts, tools, plastics, and soap. Ohio makes more steel than any other state except Indiana. Some Ohio factories make food, such as packaged meat, cookies, cheese, and pizza.

Ohio's rich soil makes it a top farming state. Soybeans and corn are the leading crops. Ohioans also raise wheat, oats, hay, and many vegetables. Apples, grapes, and strawberries thrive in Ohio, too.

Dairy cows are the state's most important farm animals. Some of their milk ends up as cheese or ice cream. Other

▲ **One of Ohio's many dairy farms**

farm animals include beef cattle, hogs, sheep, and chickens. Ohio ranks first in the United States in the production of eggs and Swiss cheese. It's number two in sherbet and number three in tomatoes.

Coal is Ohio's most valuable mineral. Miners dig it out of the earth in southeastern Ohio. Ohio leads the country in producing sandstone. The state also has a lot of oil and natural gas. The salt beds in northeastern Ohio are amazing. They could keep salt on our tables for a thousand years!

So far, we've looked at things that Ohio sells. Most Ohio workers sell services, however. They work in schools, hospitals, stores, restaurants, banks, and many other places. Like inventors, they use their special skills to help others.

Who are Ohioans? They are people of many **cultures.** Most Ohioans have European **ancestors.** Some were early settlers from Germany, Ireland, or the eastern United States. Later, people arrived from Poland, Hungary, Russia, and Italy. About one of every nine Ohioans is an African-American. Others belong to Latin American, Asian, or Middle Eastern cultures.

▲ **Many Europeans immigrated to Ohio, including this Lithuanian family.**

In 2000, more than 11 million people lived in Ohio. That made it seventh in population among all the states. About three of every four Ohioans live in or near cities. Areas in the northeast are more crowded. Columbus is the capital and the largest city. Next in size are Cleveland, Cincinnati, and Toledo.

▲ Cincinnati is Ohio's third-largest city.

Ohio has the world's largest Amish community. The Amish people are a Christian group that began in Switzerland. They teach separation from the world. They live in farming communities, dress plainly, and lead simple lives. They do not use electricity or cars. Amish people live in eastern Ohio.

Many Ohio festivals celebrate **ethnic** cultures. Native Americans hold **powwows** in several cities. German, Irish, African-American, and Hispanic people enjoy their own festivals, too.

Some cities even hold festivals for their farm products! People celebrate apples in Lebanon, grapes in Geneva,

▲ Horse-drawn carriages are common in Ohio's Amish communities.

▲ Actress Halle Berry was born and
raised in Cleveland.

and cherries in Bellevue.
Maple syrup is the star in
Oxford, Waynesville, and
Waverly. Apple butter,
pumpkins, and strawberries
all have their day.

Ohio has given us many
artists and entertainers.
They include actors Halle
Berry, Debra Winger, Paul
Newman, and Drew Carey.
Moviemaker Steven
Spielberg and author Toni
Morrison are also Ohioans.
Harriet Beecher Stowe wrote
Uncle Tom's Cabin (1852).
It showed the hardships
of slavery. Paul Laurence
Dunbar was a famous
African-American poet.

▲ **Ohio State University**

Oberlin College opened in 1833. It was the nation's first college to award degrees to women. It was also the first to accept all races. Ohio University has been around since 1804. It was the first university in the Northwest Territory. Ohio State University is in Columbus. Its football team, the Buckeyes, is top-notch. Columbus also has a professional hockey team in the National Hockey League—the Columbus Bluejackets. Basketball fans cheer for the Cleveland Cavaliers and the Cleveland Rockers.

Ohio has two professional football teams—the Cincinnati Bengals and the Cleveland Browns. Baseball fans follow the Cincinnati Reds and the Cleveland Indians. The Reds were the nation's first major-league baseball team. They have won five World Series titles so far.

▲ The Cleveland Indians play baseball at Jacobs Field.

Have you ever seen a ball rolling uphill? Have you seen rats playing basketball? It all happens at Toledo's COSI. That's short for the Center of Science and Industry. Columbus has a COSI, too. It's also full of surprises and hands-on fun.

You can be an inventor. Just visit Inventure Place in Akron. You'll use tools and machines to create your own invention. You'll also experiment with sound, magnetism, and filmmaking.

Would you like to explore an underground cave, complete with live bats? Or walk through a glacier—a giant block of ice? You'll find them at Cincinnati's Museum of Natural History and Science. The awesome **crystal** rooms in the real caves at Ohio Caverns will make you feel tiny.

Who are your favorite singers and bands? Chances are, they were inspired by musicians of the past. In Cleveland, you can learn about history's greatest rock stars. Just visit the Rock and Roll Hall of Fame. You'll see the stars' clothes, their instruments—even their report cards!

▲ Crystal formations can be found at Ohio Caverns.

In Columbus, the state capital, you can tour the state-house. Columbus's Ohio Historical Center is great to visit, too. You'll see old-time cars, lifelike Indian villages, and much more.

What was life like in the 1860s? Check out Ohio Village in Columbus. In the schoolhouse there, you'll see the students' chalkboards and schoolbooks. Then you can stroll through the village, past horse stables and shops. Costumed workers explain how they do their work.

▲ **Ohio Village gives tourists a glimpse of life in the 1860s.**

Ohio has many other living-history sites. Schoenbrunn Village was a missionary town in the 1700s. One log house there was Ohio's first schoolhouse. Zoar Village near Canton was an early German community.

▲ Schoenbrunn Village State Memorial is located in New Philadelphia.

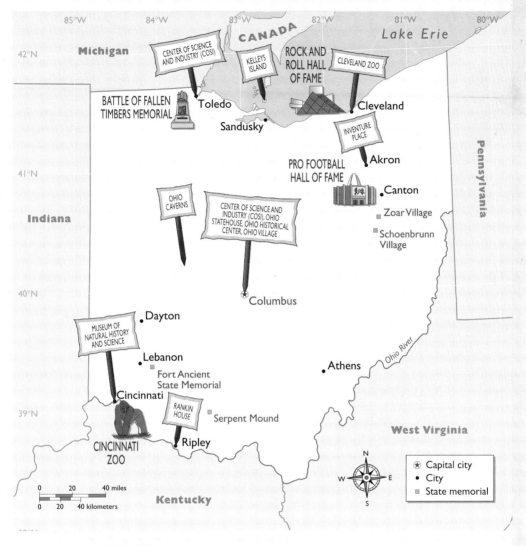

▲ Places to visit in Ohio

How did slaves hide after they escaped? You'll see at the Rankin House in Ripley. It was a safe house on the Underground Railroad. The Rankins hid slaves behind secret panels in their home.

▲ **The Pro Football Hall of Fame in Canton includes a Super Bowl Room and a revolving theater!**

Imagine a giant, winding snake that is two blocks long. That's what Serpent Mound looks like. The Adena people probably built it for religious reasons.

You'll explore Ohio's Hopewell culture at Fort Ancient. Gigantic earthen walls enclose the site. Certain spots line up with the sunrise when the seasons change.

There's much more to see in Ohio. Canton has the Pro Football Hall of Fame. Both Cincinnati and Cleveland have exciting zoos. You can tour the homes of Ohio's presidents. Or you can visit Kelleys Island in Lake Erie. **Prehistoric** Indians carved pictures on a huge rock there.

As you can see, Ohio is a great place to explore!

Important Dates

1670? La Salle is the first European to enter Ohio.

1787 The territory that will become the state of Ohio joins the United States as part of the Northwest Territory.

1788 Marietta becomes Ohio's first permanent European settlement.

1794 American Indians lose most of their Ohio lands after the Battle of Fallen Timbers.

1803 Ohio becomes the seventeenth state.

1816 Columbus becomes the state capital.

1832 The Ohio and Erie Canal connects the Ohio River and Cleveland.

1870 B. F. Goodrich begins manufacturing rubber in Akron.

1913 Hundreds of people die when Ohio's rivers flood.

1955 The Ohio Turnpike opens to traffic.

1962 Ohio astronaut John Glenn is the first American to orbit Earth.

1969 Ohioan Neil Armstrong is the first person to walk on the moon.

1977 A natural-gas shortage forces schools and businesses to close.

1985 Voters approve $100 million to reduce pollution caused by burning coal.

1993 Voters approve $200 million to reduce pollution in rivers and Lake Erie.

1996 Dayton becomes the site of the Bosnian peace talks.

2003 Ohio celebrates 200 years as a state.

Glossary

abolitionists—people who opposed slavery

ancestors—a person's grandparents, great-grandparents, and so on

astronaut—a pilot who flies in space

crystal—a mineral that lets light shine through

cultures—groups of people who share beliefs, customs, and a way of life

earthworks—structures built with soil

ethnic—relating to a nationality or culture

feather beds—mattresses stuffed with goose feathers

mounds—hills formed naturally or by humans

orbit—to move in a circle around something

powwows—Native American gatherings for meetings or ceremonies

prehistoric—living before people began to record history

slogan—a saying that represents people's beliefs

Did You Know?

★ Ohio is sometimes called the Mother of Presidents. Only the state of Virginia has produced more presidents. (Eight presidents were born in Virginia.) Seven presidents were born in Ohio. They are Ulysses S. Grant, Rutherford B. Hayes, James A. Garfield, Benjamin Harrison, William McKinley, William Howard Taft, and Warren G. Harding. Another president, William Henry Harrison, moved to Ohio as an adult.

★ Cleveland was the world's first city to have electric streetlights. The lights went on in Cleveland in 1879.

★ Roy Plunkett made life smoother. He invented a slippery material called Teflon in 1938.

★ Ohio's first capital was Chillicothe (1803–1810). Zanesville was the capital from 1810 until 1812. Columbus became the capital in 1816.

★ James Gamble of Cincinnati invented the floating bar of soap. He co-founded the Procter & Gamble Company.

★ German settlers opened the first kindergarten, in Columbus in 1838.

State capital: Columbus

State motto: With God, All Things Are Possible

State nickname: The Buckeye State

State slogan: Ohio—So Much to Discover!

Statehood: March 1, 1803; seventeenth state

Area: 41,328 square miles (107,040 sq km); **rank:** thirty-fifth

Highest point: Campbell Hill in Logan County, 1,550 feet (472 m) above sea level

Lowest point: Along the Ohio River in Hamilton County, 433 feet (132 m) above sea level

Highest recorded temperature: 113°F (45°C) near Gallipolis on July 21, 1934

Lowest recorded temperature: −39°F (−39°C) at Milligan on February 10, 1899

Average January temperature: 28°F (−2°C)

Average July temperature: 73°F (23°C)

Population in 2000: 11,353,140; **rank:** seventh

Largest cities in 2000: Columbus (711,470), Cleveland (478,403), Cincinnati (331,285), Toledo (313,619)

Factory products: Motor vehicles, metal products, chemicals, steel, machines, foods

Farm products: Soybeans, corn, milk, eggs, wheat, apples

Mining products: Coal, natural gas, oil, sandstone, limestone, salt

State flag: Ohio's state flag is the only one that's pennant-shaped. It is a long triangle with a notch in the "flapping" end. On the flagpole side is a blue triangle with seventeen stars. They stand for Ohio's place as the seventeenth state. In the center of the blue field is a white circle with a red center. The white circle is an *O,* Ohio's first letter. The red center stands for the buckeye. Red and white stripes make up the rest of the flag.

State seal: The state seal shows the sun rising over mountains. That refers to Ohio as the first state west of the Allegheny Mountains. A bundle of wheat represents Ohio's farming. Next to the wheat is a cluster of seventeen arrows. This means that Ohio was the seventeenth state.

State abbreviations: O. (traditional); OH (postal)

State Symbols

State bird: Cardinal

State flower: Scarlet carnation

State tree: Buckeye

State animal: White-tailed deer

State wildflower: Large white trillium

State reptile: Black racer (snake)

State insect: Ladybug

State beverage: Tomato juice

State gemstone: Flint

State fossil: Trilobite

State rock song: "Hang on Sloopy" by Rick Derringer

State poetry day: Third Friday of October

State commemorative quarter: released 2002

Making Ohio Maple-Apple Crunch

Maple syrup and apples are delicious Ohio products!

Makes six servings.

INGREDIENTS:

8 to 10 graham crackers

1/2 cup butter or margarine

4 apples

1/2 cup maple syrup

Ice cream (if desired)

DIRECTIONS:

Ask an adult to help with knives and hot things. Preheat oven to 325°. Crush the graham crackers and mix well with the butter. (It's easier if the butter is softened first.) Peel and slice the apples. Grease a 1-quart baking dish. Place the apple slices in the bottom. Pour maple syrup over the apple slices. Spread the graham cracker mixture on top. Bake for 25 minutes. Serve warm. Spoon ice cream on top for an extra treat.

"Beautiful Ohio"

Words by Wilbert McBride; music by Mary Earl
(earlier, original words by Ballard MacDonald)

I sailed away;
Wandered afar;
Crossed the mighty restless sea;
Looked for where I ought to be.
Cities so grand, mountains above,
Led to this land I love.

Chorus:
Beautiful Ohio, where the golden grain
Dwarf the lovely flowers in the summer rain.
Cities rising high, silhouette the sky.
Freedom is supreme in this majestic land;
Mighty factories seem to hum a tune, so grand.
Beautiful Ohio, thy wonders are in view,
Land where my dreams all come true!

Neil Armstrong (1930–) was an astronaut. In 1969, Armstrong (pictured above left) became the first person to walk on the moon.

Paul Laurence Dunbar (1872–1906) was a famous African-American poet. He was the son of escaped slaves.

Thomas Edison (1847–1931) was one of the greatest inventors ever. His inventions include electric light bulbs, record players, and motion-picture cameras.

John Glenn (1921–) became the first American astronaut to orbit Earth. In 1962, he circled Earth three times. Glenn was a U.S. senator from Ohio from 1975 to 1999.

Ulysses S. Grant (1822–1885) led the Union forces in the Civil War. He became the eighteenth U.S. president (1869–1877).

William Henry Harrison (1773–1841) fought American Indians in the Battle of Tippecanoe and the Battle of the Thames. He died of pneumonia after serving thirty days as the ninth U.S. president (1841).

William McKinley (1843–1901) was the twenty-fifth U.S. president (1897–1901). He was assassinated while in office.

Toni Morrison (1931–) is an African-American author. She won the Nobel Prize for literature in 1993.

Jesse Owens (1913–1980) was an African-American track star at Ohio State University. He won four gold medals in the 1936 Olympic Games and became one of the most famous athletes in history.

Steven Spielberg (1946–) is one of the world's great moviemakers. He made *E.T., the Extra-Terrestrial* (1982), *Schindler's List* (1993), the "Indiana Jones" movies, and many others.

Harriet Beecher Stowe (1811–1896) wrote *Uncle Tom's Cabin* (1852). It describes the hardships of slavery and intensified the disagreement that led to the Civil War.

William Howard Taft (1857–1930) was the twenty-seventh U.S. president (1909–1913). He went on to become chief justice of the U.S. Supreme Court (1921–1930).

Tecumseh (1768–1813) was a famous Shawnee chief who fought to defend Indian lands from white people. He was killed in battle.

Want to Know More?

At the Library

Joseph, Paul. *Ohio*. Edina, Minn.: Abdo & Daughters, 1998.

Kline, Nancy. *Ohio*. Danbury, Conn.: Children's Press, 2002.

Lewis, J. Patrick, and Chris Sheban. *The Shoe Tree of Chagrin*. Mankato, Minn.: Creative Editions, 2001.

Lutz, Norma Jean. *Escape from Slavery*. Broomall, Pa.: Chelsea House, 1999.

Van Leeuwen, Jean, and Phil Boatwright. *Nothing Here but Trees*. New York: Dial Books for Young Readers, 1998.

Wills, Patricia. *Danger Along the Ohio*. New York: Clarion Books, 1997.

On the Web

Ohio

http://www.ohio.gov/
For information on Ohio's government, economy, and landmarks

Ohio Tourism

http://www.ohiotourism.com
For a look at Ohio's events, activities, and interesting sights

Through the Mail

Ohio Division of Travel and Tourism

P.O. Box 1001
Columbus, OH 43266
For information on travel and interesting sights in Ohio

Ohio Secretary of State

30 East Broad Street
14th Floor
Columbus, OH 43266
For information on Ohio's government

On the Road

Ohio Statehouse

Broad and High Streets
Columbus, OH 43215
614/728-2695
To visit Ohio's state capitol

Ohio Historical Center

1982 Velma Avenue
Columbus, OH 43211
614/297-2357 or 800/797-2357
To see interesting exhibits on Ohio's history

Index

About the Author

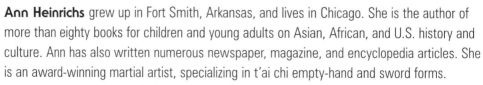

Ann Heinrichs grew up in Fort Smith, Arkansas, and lives in Chicago. She is the author of more than eighty books for children and young adults on Asian, African, and U.S. history and culture. Ann has also written numerous newspaper, magazine, and encyclopedia articles. She is an award-winning martial artist, specializing in t'ai chi empty-hand and sword forms.

Ann has traveled widely throughout the United States, Africa, Asia, and the Middle East. In exploring each state for this series, she rediscovered the people, history, and resources that make this a great land, as well as the concerns we share with people around the world.